Homemade Protein Bars

Healthy, Fast & Delicious Protein Bar Recipes You Can Make at Home

By: Owen Davis

Copyright Notice!

Table of Contents

Introduction

There is nothing better than a homemade protein bar recipe. They are easy to make and let you enjoy the benefits of eating healthy without going through all the hassle. Protein bar recipes are great to have in your kitchen so that you can keep them on hand for the days when you need a quick treat.

While helpful, protein bars should only be considered a supplementary component of your diet. Protein bars as the main source can deny you the benefits of the much-needed minerals, vitamins, fiber, healthy fats, and phytochemicals abundant in other foods. As long you have a healthy and balanced diet, consuming protein bars shouldn't need to be a daily occurrence. Your main focus should be nutrition and proper exercise. Protein bars are the best choice if you are looking for a product to help you lose weight, gain muscle, or add more protein to your diet without the added calories. But only use them as a supplement and not as a meal.

Some protein powders can contain as much protein as your regular chicken breast. Most manufacturers of protein powders use soy or whey protein as main ingredients. Those who want to avoid soy or whey protein for health reasons can opt for plant-based protein powders. Manufacturers of plant-based protein powders use hemp and rice as the main ingredient. n Some are even gluten-free, making them suitable for people who have a gluten allergy.

There are many homemade protein bars recipes to choose from, but if you want to make healthy and delicious with no preservatives found in protein bars at home, then all you need is creativity and the right ingredients. This book features the best protein bar recipes that combine healthy and tasty ingredients.

All the recipes are designed for convenience; you only need a few minutes to make them.

Chapter 1 The Benefits of a High Protein Diet

The benefits of a high protein diet are apparent, leading us to ask this question: how much should we consume? This number depends completely on your weight and activity level. Experts agree that you should eat between ½ and 1 gram of protein for each pound of your body weight.

This means that if you're a 140-pound woman who exercises lightly, you should eat approximately seventy grams of protein daily. If you're a 140-pound woman who exercises frequently, you will want to increase that protein intake, riding closer to 140. If you achieve the proper amount of protein in your diet, you can expect real, physical, and mental changes in your body. Look to the following information for a better understanding.

1. Repair Muscles and Power Your Day

As you live and work, your body's muscles are undergoing a ceaseless cycle of muscle loss and muscle gain. Destruction, construction, and repair. Depending on your activity level and whether or not your body has enough amino acids (found readily in animal-based and plant-based proteins), you can end up losing more than you gain—and fast. If you exert and strain your muscles without the requisite amount of protein in your system being converted into those precious amino acids, muscle degeneration is a certainty—which ultimately forces your metabolism to falter. Providing your body with protein, and the right kinds, encourages this protein synthesis and keeps you going, rather than withering away.

Learn the right kinds of proteins you need, and the very specific benefits protein has on your muscles, on your mind as you live and work each day. Keep in mind that moving toward a high-protein diet is absolutely essential for re-growth.

2. Build Up Muscle Mass

High protein intake allows for muscle mass gain, which can both slenderize your body and rev your metabolism. Furthermore, when you pair a high-protein diet with exercise and weightlifting, the complete amino acid formula found in complete protein sources allows you to repair from muscle damage. This means you can get back out there and continue to build.

3. Maintain Bone Mass

 Some of the nine amino acids derived from proteins are used to build and strengthen your bones. This is important to reduce your risk of osteoporosis and keep you strong and lean. Many protein rich foods and recipes include high amount of calcium, as well, which also assists with bone strength and growth.

4. Improve Mental Function

A high protein diet gives you improved brain performance. Because it activates many of your neuroreceptors in your mind, it improves alertness and memory—drawing connections from cell to cell that allow your brain to "access" information.

5. Decrease the Frequency of Hunger Pangs

Eating a high protein diet is the best way to feel fuller for longer, allowing you to feel satisfied without taking in too many carbohydrates and calories—which all lead to weight gain. Furthermore, a high protein diet turns you away from daily snacks, allowing your body to heal between meals—something that can only occur if you give your kidney and liver a break from caloric intake.

6. Improve Your Energy Levels

Protein is a macronutrient. This means that it quickly converts to energy, without much cellular waste. A diet high in protein intake improves your energy efficiency. As such, your body rewards you with high energy levels and alertness for the rest of your day.

7. Lose Fat, and Fast

A protein rich diet works to satiate you so well that you automatically decrease your desire for added snacks. You'll automatically reduce your calorie intake, which works to help you achieve a fitter body. Also, restricting your carb intake means that you intake less sugar, which automatically converts to glucose in your body. When your diet is high in carbohydrates, you further decrease your chance of weight loss because the insulin in your system disallows your body to utilize fat for energy.

Furthermore, eating a diet high in protein is perfect for day-of weight loss, as it eliminates bloating and water weight.

8. Finally Get Some Good, Quality Sleep

Eating lots of protein helps you sleep better during the night. This is because a high protein diet ensures proper neurotransmitter production. Neurotransmitters both regulate your sleep cycle and keep you active and awake throughout the day—something that has necessarily fallen away from our society because of our house lights, our air conditioning, and our confusing, anti-biological lifestyles. However, healthy neurotransmitters allow us to retreat back to this healthy lifestyle.

Chapter 2 Recipes

1. Chocolate Strawberry Protein Bars

This bar is the perfect replacement for chocolate-dipped strawberries. Although, to be honest, nothing quite compares to the latter.

Preparation Time: 15 Minutes

Servings: 10

Ingredients

- 1/2 cup strawberry protein powder
- 1/3 cup almond flour
- 2/3 cup coconut milk
- 1/2 dark white chocolate chips

Directions

Stir together the protein powder and almond flour.

Add the coconut milk one tablespoon at a time until the mixture comes together.

Shape into 10 bars. Freeze bars for 15 minutes to firm up.

Melt the chocolate and pour it over the top of the bars.

Refrigerate bars until the chocolate sets.

2. Chocolate Almond Protein Bars

A decadent snack after an intense workout.

Preparation Time: 10 Minutes

Servings: 8

Ingredients

- 2/3 cup coconut flour
- 1/4 cup chocolate protein powder
- 1/4 cup almond butter
- 1/4 cup applesauce
- 3 tablespoons honey
- 3 tablespoons almond milk
- 1 teaspoon vanilla extract
- 1/4 cup chocolate chips

Directions

Preheat oven to 350°

Line a loaf pan with baking paper.

Mix the coconut flour and protein powder together.

Place almond butter, applesauce, honey, almond milk, and vanilla extract in a microwave-safe bowl. Microwave for 10 seconds, then stir the mixture until smooth.

Combine the wet ingredients and dry ingredients until a dough forms.

Mix in chocolate chips.

Transfer the mixture to a loaf pan and press down to create an even surface.

Bake for 10 minutes. Allow to cool, then cut into 8 bars.

3. Chocolate Cranberry Protein Bars

A crunchy bar with chocolate, cranberries, and quinoa.

Preparation Time: 20 Minutes

Servings: 8

Ingredients

- 1 cup dried cranberries
- 1 tablespoon water
- 1 cup almonds, halved
- 1/2 cup seeds, your choice
- 1/2 cup popped quinoa
- 2 tablespoons maple syrup
- 1/4 cup chocolate chips

Directions

Line a loaf pan with wax paper.

Blend the cranberries and water into a paste.

Combine the paste and all the other ingredients (except chocolate chips).

Refrigerate bars overnight.

Melt the choc chips and drizzle over the mixture.

Refrigerate the mixture until the chocolate is set. Cut into 8 bars.

4. Cherry Pistachio Protein Bars

Luxurious cherries and pistachios give a feeling of Christmas. Use cherries soaked in liquor for a festive kick.

Preparation Time: 45 Minutes

Servings: 8

Ingredients

- 2 cups pistachios, halved
- 2/3 cup popped quinoa
- 2/3 cup cherries, chopped
- 1/2 cup shredded coconut
- 2/3 cup maple syrup

Directions

Line an 8x8 inch pan with wax paper.

Mix the pistachios, quinoa, cherries, and coconut together.

Heat the maple syrup slightly and pour over the dry mix. Stir in quickly.

Transfer mix to pan and press down until the surface is smooth.

Refrigerate bars for 30 minutes.

Cut into 8 bars.

5. Spicy Chai Protein Bars

These bars taste similar to Chai tea and are perfect when running errands.

Preparation Time: 25 Minutes

Servings: 9

Ingredients

- 1 and 1/2 cups coconut flour
- 2 tablespoons plant-based protein powder
- 2 tablespoons brown sugar
- 1 teaspoon baking soda
- 1 teaspoon cinnamon and allspice
- 1/2 teaspoon cardamom, nutmeg
- 2 large eggs
- 1/2 cup honey
- 2 tablespoons melted coconut oil

Directions

Line an 8x 8 inch pan with baking paper.

Preheat oven to 350°

Mix dry ingredients in a large bowl.

Whisk together wet ingredients.

Add wet ingredients to dry ingredients and stir well.

Transfer mixture to the pan and smooth surface with a spatula.

Bake for 15 minutes.

Allow to cool, then cut into bars.

6. Green Tea Protein Bars

Green tea has a wide variety of health and weight loss benefits. As with every other bar, this one has high protein and is without nasty grains.

Preparation Time: 30 Minutes

Servings: 8

Ingredients

- 1 cup quick oats
- 1 and 1/2 cups almond flour
- 1/2 cup shredded coconut
- 1 tablespoon green tea powder
- 2 tablespoons vanilla protein powder
- 1 cup almond butter, melted
- 3 cups almond milk

Directions

Line a loaf pan with wax paper.

Mix the dry ingredients together until well combined.

Add the almond butter to the dry ingredients and combine.

Add the almond milk and mix until very well combined.

Transfer mixture to loaf pan and press down until the surface is even.

Refrigerate 30 minutes. Cut into bars.

7. Lime Protein Bars

Tart and refreshing – perfect for a hot day!

Preparation Time: 45 Minutes

Servings: 9

Ingredients

- 1 cup coconut flour
- 1/2 cup vanilla protein powder
- 1/2 teaspoon baking soda
- 6 oz lime juice
- 1 tablespoon lime zest
- 4 egg whites
- 1/2 teaspoon stevia
- 8 oz unsweetened applesauce

Directions

Line an 8 x 8 inch pan with baking paper.

Preheat the oven to 350°

Mix the dry ingredients in a bowl.

Mix the wet ingredients in a bowl.

Add the wet ingredients to the dry ingredients and mix thoroughly.

Transfer the mixture to the pan and spread evenly with a spatula.

Bake for 25 minutes.

Allow to cool then slice into bars.

8. Pea-Nut Protein Bar

This bar should fuel you for several hours, packed with nuts and chickpeas.

Preparation Time: 30 Minutes

Servings: 10

Ingredients

- 15 oz chickpeas, washed
- 1/2 cup soft dates, packed
- 1/4 cup nut butter
- 1 teaspoon almond extract
- 1/4 teaspoon Himalayan rock salt
- 2/3 cup protein powder
- 1/3 cup chopped nuts
- 1/3 cup dried fruit

Directions

Line a large loaf pan with wax paper.

Combine chickpeas, dates, nut butter, almond extract, and salt in a food processor. Scrape down sides of the bowl as necessary.

Add protein powder, nuts, and dried fruit to the mixture. Use the pulse setting to combine ingredients until the dough forms a ball.

Transfer the mixture to the pan and press down to form an even surface.

Refrigerate 5 hours. Remove from pan and cut into bars.

9. Seed Krispie Protein Bars

These bars are an adult version of Rice Krispie treats but healthy enough for kids as well.

Preparation Time: 25 Minutes

Servings: 8

Ingredients

- 1/2 cup Rice Krispies
- 2/3 cup mixed seeds
- 1 cup oats
- 1/4 teaspoon salt
- 1 teaspoon cinnamon and cardamom
- 1/2 cup nuts, chopped
- 1/3 cup maple syrup
- 1/2 cup nut butter

Directions

Preheat the oven to 350°

Line an 8 x 8 inch pan with baking paper.

Combine dry ingredients in a large bowl.

Microwave syrup and nut butter until soft.

Add wet ingredients to dry ingredients and combine well, using hands if necessary.

Transfer mixture to pan and press down to create an even surface.

Bake bars for 15 minutes.

Allow to cool and then slice into bars.

10. Kiddies Protein Bars

A snack is as good as candy and perfect for kids.

Preparation Time: 25 Minutes

Servings: 12

Ingredients

- 4 cups cereal – preferably granola
- 1/2 cup chocolate protein powder
- 2 tablespoons semi-sweet chocolate chips
- 1/2 cup mini marshmallows
- 1/4 cup peanut butter
- 1 tablespoon. coconut oil

Directions

Line an 8 x 8 inch pan with wax paper.

Mix cereal, protein powder, chocolate chips, and marshmallows together.

Heat peanut butter, coconut oil, and honey in the microwave till just boiling.

Pour syrup over cereal mix and stir until well combined.

Transfer mixture to pan and press down to form an even surface.

Refrigerate for 40 minutes then cut into bars.

11. Chewy Muesli Protein Bars

A bar suitable for breakfast or a snack.

Preparation Time: 20 Minutes

Servings: 12

Ingredients

- 6 oz muesli (your choice)
- 1/2 cup protein powder
- 2 tablespoons ground flax seeds
- 1 teaspoon ground cinnamon
- 1/4 teaspoon salt
- 1/4 cup nut butter
- 1/4 cup maple syrup
- 1/2 cup coconut milk
- 1 teaspoon vanilla extract
- 1/3 cup chocolate chips

Directions

Preheat oven to 350°

Line an 8 x 8 inch pan with baking paper.

Combine dry ingredients in one bowl.

Combine wet ingredients in another bowl.

Mix wet ingredients into dry ingredients until well combined.

Mix in chocolate chips.

Transfer mixture to pan and press down to form an even surface,

Bake for 20 minutes.

Allow to cool, then cut into bars.

12. Birthday Cake Protein Bars

Who doesn't love sprinkles? Enjoy this as a special birthday treat. Or better – cook them up for someone else's birthday.

Preparation Time: 30 Minutes

Servings: 12

Ingredients

- 3 cups almond flour
- 1/2 cup vanilla protein powder
- 1 teaspoon stevia
- A pinch of salt
- 1/4 cup nut butter
- 1/2 cup maple syrup
- 1 tablespoon vanilla extract
- 2/3 cup almond milk
- 2 tablespoons sprinkles

Directions

Line an 8 x 8 inch pan with wax paper.

Mix together flour, protein powder, stevia, and salt.

In a microwave-safe bowl, combine nut butter and syrup. Heat till melted and stir into a smooth mixture.

Add wet mix to dry mix and stir until well combined, approximately 2 minutes.

Add vanilla, almond milk, and sprinkles to the mixture and combine well.

Transfer mixture to pan and press down to form a smooth surface.

Refrigerate 30 minutes then cut into bars.

13. Rocky Road Protein Bars

A wonderful, chewy treat packed with protein.

Preparation Time: 45 Minutes

Servings: 9

Ingredients

- 1 cup coconut flour
- 1/2 cup shredded coconut
- 1 cup graham crackers, crushed
- 1/4 cup chocolate protein powder
- 1/2 cup peanut butter, melted
- 1/3 cup maple syrup
- 1/4 cup coconut milk
- 1/2 cup mini marshmallows
- 1/2 cup chocolate chips
- 1/4 cup chopped nuts

Directions

Line an 8 x 8 inch pan with wax paper.

Mix together coconut flour, coconut, graham crackers, and protein powder.

Stir together peanut butter and maple syrup. Microwave 10 seconds to make a smooth mixture.

Mix the wet ingredients into the dry ingredients using your hands to form a crumbly dough

Mix in the coconut milk till well combined.

Add the marshmallows, chocolate chips, and nuts and knead into the mixture.

Transfer mixture to pan and press to create an even surface.

Refrigerate 45 minutes, then cut into bars.

14. Chocolate Chai Protein Bars

Chia seeds are very healthy, and these bars are good for any occasion.

Preparation Time: 30 Minutes

Servings: 12

Ingredients

- 14 soft dates, pitted
- 1 tablespoon water
- 1 cup nut butter
- 1/4 cup almond milk
- 2 cups oats
- 1/2 cup chocolate protein powder
- 1/3 cup chia seeds
- 1/4 cup cocoa
- 1/4 cup chocolate sprinkles

Directions

Line a 9 x 9 inch pan with wax paper.

Use a blender to create a smooth paste from the dates and water.

Add in peanut butter and milk and blend briefly.

Mix nut butter, oats, protein powder, chai seeds, and cocoa in a large bowl.

Add the wet ingredients to the dry ingredients and mix well.

Transfer mixture to pan and press down to create an even surface.

Press sprinkles onto the top of mixture.

Refrigerate for 30 minutes then cut into bars.

15. Thanksgiving Protein Bars

A healthy bar to be thankful for on Thanksgiving. There's no turkey in it – sorry to disappoint.

Preparation Time: 40 Minutes

Servings: 12

Ingredients

- 1 and 1/2 cups fresh pumpkin, pureed
- 6 egg whites
- 3 tablespoons honey
- 1 teaspoon vanilla extract
- 1 teaspoon stevia
- 1/4 cup protein powder
- 2 tablespoons brown sugar
- 2 tablespoons mixed spice or pumpkin pie spice
- 1 cup quick oats
- 1/3 cup walnuts, chopped

Directions

Line an 8 x 8 inch pan with baking paper.

Preheat the oven to 350°

Mix together pumpkin, egg whites, honey, vanilla extract, and stevia until well combined.

In a separate bowl, mix together protein powder, brown sugar, and spices. Add the quick oats and mix well.

Transfer mixture to pan and smooth the surface with a spatula.

Sprinkle walnuts over the top and drizzle with honey if desired.

Bake for 40 minutes. Remove from oven and allow to cool, then slice into bars.

16. Very Berry Protein Bars

A fruitful snack bar packed with berries.

Preparation Time: 30 Minutes

Servings: 6

Ingredients

- 5 oz frozen mixed berries
- 2 oz shredded coconut
- 2 oz vanilla protein powder
- 1 teaspoon vanilla extract
- 1/4 cup almond milk

Directions

Line a loaf pan with wax paper.

Use a food processor to pulp berries.

Add coconut, protein powder, and vanilla and pulse briefly to create crumbs.

Add in almond milk and process until the mixture starts to form a dough.

Transfer to pan and press down to create an even surface.

Refrigerate for 30 minutes then cut into bars.

17. Ginger Flake Protein Bars

Crystallized ginger provides an interesting flavor-alternative to traditional protein bars.

Preparation Time: 20 Minutes

Servings: 10

Ingredients

- 2 tablespoons nut butter
- 1/4 cup maple syrup
- 1/4 cup almond milk
- 2 scoops protein powder
- 1 cup quick oats
- 1 cup Bran flakes, crushed
- 1/2 cup almonds, chopped
- 1/4 cup mixed seeds
- 1/2 cup crystallized ginger, chopped
- 1/4 cup shredded coconut

Directions

Preheat the oven to 325°

Line a 9 x 9 inch pan with baking paper.

In a microwave-safe cup, mix together nut butter and maple syrup. Microwave until melted.

Add milk and protein powder and mix till smooth.

In a separate bowl, mix together oats, bran flakes, almonds, ginger, seeds, and coconut.

Add wet ingredients to dry ingredients and mix till well combined.

Bake for 20 minutes. Remove from oven and cut into bars when completely cool.

18. Fruit Coconut Protein Bars

Many different kinds of fruit and coconut go great together. Coconut goes great with strawberries, pineapples, mango, bananas, and more.

Preparation Time: 25 Minutes

Servings: 10

Ingredients:

- 60 grams of the fruit of your choice
- 60 grams of shredded coconut
- 60 grams of protein powder (or wheat germ)
- 1/2 a teaspoon of vanilla
- 60 milliliters of almond milk
- 80 grams of dark chocolate

Directions:

Take your fruit and grind them up in a blender or processor.

Add the coconut, wheat germ (or protein powder), and vanilla, and mix the entire mixture until it is quite fine.

Add in the almond milk and process it until the mixture completely comes together.

Line a pan with wax paper and put the mixture evenly into the pan.

At this point, put the mixture into the fridge and leave it there until it completely hardens. Once it has, you can cut out the bars that you want.

Once you have cut out the bars, microwave the dark chocolate, and when it is melted, you can put it over top of the bars that you have just cut out. Let the chocolate set completely, then serve and enjoy.

19. No-Bake Rice Krispy Treats Bar

Rice crispy treats are a classic treat. This recipe cuts down on the calories yet still tastes great and is easy to make.

Preparation Time: 20 Minutes

Servings: 10

Ingredients:

- 1 and 1/2 cups of rolled oats
- 1/2 a cup of wheat germ
- 1/2 a cup of rice krispy cereal
- 1/2 a teaspoon of salt
- 1/2 a cup of peanut butter
- 1/2 a cup of maple syrup
- 1 teaspoon of vanilla extract
- 3 tablespoons on chocolate chips
- 1/2 a tablespoon of coconut oil

Directions:

Take an 8 x 8 inch pan and line it with parchment paper.

Mix the oats, wheat germ, rice krispy cereal, and salt.

Put in the peanut butter, syrup, and vanilla extract.

Combine very well, adding water or milk as needed if it is too dry.

Press into a pan and make sure it is smooth.

At this point, you can put it in the freezer and leave it there for roughly one hour.

Melt the chocolate chips and oil together on low-heat. Stir until it is smooth.

Once the bars are frozen, remove them from the freezer and slice them into

Put the chocolate over the top and freeze until set.

20. German Chocolate Bar

This rich dark chocolate bar is combined with crunchy coconut and pecan.

Preparation Time: 25 Minutes

Servings: 10

Ingredients:

- 1 cup of oats
- 1/2 a cup of soy protein
- 1/4 cup of cocoa powder
- 2/3 of a cup of dates
- 1/3 of a cup of pecans
- 1/2 a cup of coconut
- 2 tablespoons of rice syrup
- 1 teaspoon of vanilla extract
- 1/2 a pinch of salt

Directions:

With a food processor or blender, grind up the oats into a fine powder.

Add in the cocoa powder and the soy protein. Make sure everything is combined well.

Rinse the dates and put them into the processor with pecans, coconut, syrup, vanilla, and salt.

Blend well and add water as needed until dough begins to form.

Put the dough into a bowl and put the chocolate chips into the dough.

Put the dough out onto some parchment paper that is on a baking mat.

Cover with another piece of paper and roll out so that the bars are roughly a half inch thick. Make sure that the dough is in a square shape.

Put the bar mixture into the fridge for two to three hours.

21. Raw Pumpkin Bars

It doesn't have to be Halloween for you to enjoy these pumpkin bars.

Preparation Time: 35 Minutes

Servings: 10

Ingredients:

- 1/2 a cup of dates
- 1/4 a cup of water
- 1/2 a cup of hemp butter
- 2 cups of oats
- 1/4 cup of pumpkin seeds
- 2 tablespoons of chia seeds
- 1/2 a teaspoon of vanilla extract
- 1/2 a teaspoon of cinnamon
- 1/4 a teaspoon of nutmeg
- 1/4 a teaspoon of salt

Directions:

Line a baking pan with parchment paper.

Soak the dates in the water for 30 minutes and then transfer to a blender and blend until they are nothing but a paste.

Pour the paste into a bowl and add the hemp butter and combine.

Put in the remaining ingredients and mix well.

Put it into a baking sheet and be sure to spread it out, so it's flat and even.

Put in the fridge and leave it there for two hours.

22. Maca Bars

Maca is a root that's originally from Peru. It's known for enhancing energy and is often referred to as "The Peruvian Ginseng." This is an excellent bar to eat before you hit the gym.

Preparation Time: 30 Minutes

Servings: 10

Ingredients:

- 1 cup of almonds
- 1/2 a cup of sunflower seeds
- 1/2 a cup of flax meal
- 1/2 a cup of pepitas
- 2 tablespoons of chia seeds
- 2 tablespoons of maca powder
- 1/4 cup of maple syrup
- 1/4 cup of coconut oil
- 1/3 of a cup of almond butter
- 1/2 a teaspoon of salt

Directions:

Take the almonds, put them in a blender or processor, and grind them until they are course.

Add the almonds into a bowl with sunflower seeds, maca powder, chia seeds, salt, flax meal, and pepitas.

In a saucepan, combine the syrup, butter, and oil and mix until well combined.

Add the wet mixture to the dry mixture. Mix it together.

Put it in an 8 x 8 inch pan lined with parchment paper.

Spread over the mixture and make sure it is flat and packed tight.

Put in the fridge for one hour.

23. Easy Peanut Butter Bar

This recipe is really easy to make.

Preparation Time: 45 Minutes

Servings: 10

Ingredients:

- 4 and 1/2 cups of oatmeal
- 1 and 1/3 cups of peanut butter
- 1 cup of milk
- 5 scoops of wheat germ

Directions

Combine wheat germ, milk, and peanut butter and mix well.

Add in the oatmeal and mix it together well.

Flatten it into a dish and put it in the fridge. It should stay in the fridge for about two hours.

24. Chocolate Peanut Butter Bars

Chocolate combined with peanut butter makes for a gooey, tasty treat.

Preparation Time:

Servings: 10

Ingredients:

- 1 cup of rolled oats
- 8 scoops of brown rice powder
- 5 tablespoons of a sweetener of your choice
- 3 tablespoons of dark cocoa powder
- 1/8 of a teaspoon of salt
- 1/2 of peanut butter
- 1 cup and 2 tablespoons of almond milk

Directions:

Take 9-inch brownie pan and cover it with parchment paper.

Take the oats and blend them in a processor until they are mostly just powder and put them in a large bowl.

Add the brown rice powder, sweetener, salt, and cocoa, and then put aside.

In another large bowl, combine the peanut butter and the milk.

Add the dry ingredients with the wet ingredients. Form it all into one big dough ball.

Knead the dough until it is flat and place it into the brownie pan.

Cover the pan in a plastic wrap and put it in the fridge overnight.

25. Cookie Dough Protein Bars

Sometimes you just want to eat a bowl of cookie dough. This recipe will help fix that craving.

Preparation Time: 30 Minutes

Servings: 10

Ingredients:

- 1 and 1/2 cups of rolled oats
- 1/2 of raw almond butter
- 1 cup of almond milk
- 5 tablespoons of a sweetener of your choice
- 1/2 a teaspoon of butter flavor
- 1/2 a teaspoon of stevia extract
- 1/4 teaspoon of salt
- 1/4 cup of brown rice flour
- 8 scoops of brown rice protein powder
- 1/3 of a cup of chocolate chips

Directions:

Take a baking pan (8- or 9-inch) and line it with parchment paper.

Blend the oats into powder.

In a large bowl, combine the almond butter and almond milk together.

Add the sweetener, stevia, butter extract, and salt and mix it all together.

Add in the brown rice flour and the oat flour.

Add in the brown rice protein powder, which will thicken the dough to resemble cookie dough.

Take the chocolate chips and mix them into the dough.

Put the entire mixture into the baking pan and flatten it so that it is smooth on the top.

Cover it over with plastic wrap and put it in the fridge, where it will remain overnight.

26. Snickers Protein Bar

You'll feel truly satisfied after eating this layered bar.

Preparation Time: 45 Minutes

Servings: 10

Ingredients:

- 1/2 cup peanut butter
- 1 cup almond milk
- 1/4 teaspoon salt
- 2/3 cup oat flour
- 10 scoops vanilla protein powder
- 1 and 1/2 teaspoons sweetener
- 1/2 cup Walden Farm's caramel syrup (0 calorie)
- 2 tablespoons peanut flour
- 1/2 cup roasted, unsalted peanuts
- 9 ounces dark chocolate

Directions:

Make the Protein Base

In a bowl, mix the peanut butter, almond milk, and salt.

In another bowl, whisk the oat flour and 8 scoops of protein powder together.

Add the oat flour and protein powder to the wet mixture.

Take the mixture, spread it into a pan, and put it in the fridge for at least 2 hours.

Make the caramel topping

Mix the syrup, 2 scoops of protein powder, sweetener, and the peanut flour in a bowl.

Scoop and spread the mixture over the protein bar base.

Put in the refrigerator for at least 30 minutes

Make the chocolate coating

Put the chocolate in a double boiler.

Dip the protein bars in the melted chocolate. Drip off the excess chocolate.

Refrigerate for at least 2 hours.

27. Maca Energy Bars

Maca is a root powder that contains high amounts of vitamin B. It also includes a lot of energy to sustain you after your exercise. Almonds, flax, and sunflower seeds are added to boost the protein content of this energy bar.

Preparation Time: 30 Minutes

Servings: 10

Ingredients:

- 1/2 teaspoon sea salt
- 1/3 cup almond butter
- 1/4 cup coconut oil
- 1/4 cup maple syrup
- 2 tablespoons maca powder
- 2 tablespoons chia seeds
- 1/2 cup pepitas
- 1/2 cup flax meal
- 1/2 cup sunflower seeds
- 1 cup almonds

Directions:

Grind the almonds in the food processor until you form a coarse consistency.

Scoop in a mixing bowl and add the maca powder, sunflower seeds, pepitas, flax meal, salt, and chia seeds.

In a saucepan, mix the almond butter, coconut oil, and maple syrup.

Add the maple mixture to the almond mixture. Fold in to combine all ingredients.

Pour the batter on to a baking pan lined with parchment paper.

Place in a fridge for an hour before slicing into bars.

28. Chocolate Protein Bars

This is a simple protein recipe bar that is very easy to make. It also contains different ingredients that are great sources of vitamins and protein.

Preparation Time: 25 Minutes

Servings: 10

Ingredients:

- A cup of mixed nuts, coconut flakes or anything that you have
- 1/2 cup chocolate whey protein
- 1/3 cup dried fruit
- 1/4 cup cacao powder
- 1/4 cup flaxseed
- 1/4 cup almond flour
- 2 small ripe bananas

Directions:

Preheat the oven to 300°

In a mixing bowl, mash the bananas and add in the flaxseed, almond flour, whey, and cacao powder. Add in the dried fruits and the mixed nuts.

Grease a baking sheet and spread the mixture evenly until 1/2 inch thick.

Bake for 25 minutes or until firm.

Cut into bite-size squares.

29. Quinoa Protein Bars

Quinoa is a good source of protein and adding peanut butter to this protein bar recipe can amp up the protein profile of the snack. The addition of chocolate also improves the antioxidant qualities of this protein bar recipe.

Preparation Time: 15 Minutes

Servings: 10

Ingredients:

- 1 tablespoon honey
- 1/4 cup dark chocolate
- 1/3 cup natural peanut butter
- 1/2 cup sliced almonds, blanched
- 16 dates, pitted
- 2/3 cup water
- 1/3 cup quinoa

Directions:

Rinse the quinoa and sieve in a strainer. Add 2/3 cup of water to a saucepan and bring to boil. Cook the quinoa for 15 minutes. Let it cool.

Place the dates inside a food processor and pulse until it forms a ball. Transfer to a mixing bowl.

In the food processor, add the almonds and mince. Be careful not to turn it into almond meal.

Leave the almond in the food processor and add the cooled quinoa. Add the peanut butter in and pulse until well blended.

Use your hands and shape the mixture into 8 small bars.

In a saucepan, add chocolates and honey and heat over low heat. Stir frequently until the chocolate is melted.

Spread the chocolate over the bar and let it cool before serving.

30. Protein Bar Brownies

This brownie recipe is adapted to become healthy food. With healthy ingredients like Greek yogurt and chocolate protein powder, this is one brownie recipe you should eat after every workout.

Preparation Time: 25 Minutes

Servings: 10

Ingredients:

- 1/4 cup whole wheat flour
- 1 teaspoon baking powder
- 1 egg
- 1/2 cup + 2 tablespoons chocolate protein powder
- 1/2 cup unsweetened cocoa powder
- 1/3 cup honey
- 1/4 cup skim milk
- 3/4 + 1/2 cup plain non-fat Greek yogurt
- 2 tablespoons coconut sugar
- 2 tablespoons unsweetened cocoa powder
- 2 tablespoons peanut butter

Directions:

Preheat the oven to 350°

To make the brownies, mix together milk, 3/4 cup yogurt, honey, and egg in a mixing bowl. Add the 1/2 cup cocoa powder, protein powder, flour, and baking powder.

Pour the batter into a greased baking pan and bake for 25 minutes.

Let it cool.

Meanwhile, prepare the frosting by mixing the remaining ingredients.

Spread the frosting on top of the cooled brownies.

31. Salted Walnut and Date Protein Bars

This protein bar is a combination of sweet and salty. It is a great snack to eat after a workout to provide you with muscle repairing abilities.

Preparation Time: 30 minutes

Servings: 10

Ingredients:

- 1/8 teaspoon sea salt
- 6 tablespoons protein powder
- 3 tablespoons chopped walnuts
- 1/4 cup chopped medjool dates
- 1/2 cup oats
- 1 tsp vanilla extract
- 1/4 cup maple syrup
- 1/2 cup natural almond butter

Directions:

In a medium-sized bowl, mix together maple syrup, sea salt, vanilla, dates, and almond butter.

Add the oats, protein powder, and walnuts and mix again.

Press the mixture into a baking pan.

Refrigerate for more than an hour and cut into bars.

32. Crunchy Peanut Butter Protein Bars

This protein bar has an interesting crunch to them. It is also made with other ingredients that add goodness to the entire recipe.

Preparation Time: 30 Minutes

Servings: 10

Ingredients:

- 1/3 cup chopped peanuts
- 1 bar (43g) maca chocolate
- 1/2 cup brown rice crisp cereal
- 1/4 teaspoon salt
- 1 cup protein powder
- 10 Medjool dates, pitted
- 1/2 cup applesauce
- 1/2 cup peanut butter

Directions:

Put the applesauce, peanut butter, and dates in the food processor and pulse until smooth.

Add the protein powder and pulse until the mixture forms a dough.

Add the rice crisps and salt, and process until combined.

Line a baking dish with plastic wrap and press down the mixture.

Top with peanuts and chocolates

Refrigerate for one hour before cutting into bars.

33. Protein Bar Rice Krispy Treats

This protein bar recipe tastes better and more nutritious than your usual Rice Krispy Treats. This recipe is great because it is fortified with protein, but they taste just like the real thing you see in supermarkets – only they are more nutritious.

Preparation Time: 30 Minutes

Servings: 10

Ingredients:

- 1/2 cup mix-ins (raisins, chopped nuts)
- 5 and 1/2 cups rice krispies
- 1/2 cup protein powder
- 1 teaspoon vanilla
- 1/2 cup peanut butter
- 6 cups marshmallows
- 4 tablespoons coconut oil

Directions:

Pour the rice krispies and mix-ins of your choice into a large mixing bowl. Set aside.

In a saucepan, melt the peanut butter and coconut oil and boil over medium heat.

Turn the heat to low and add the marshmallows until melted.

Add the protein powder and vanilla.

Turn off the heat and stir. Grease a baking pan and press the mixture on the pan with greased hands.

Allow to cool before cutting into bars.

34. Blueberry Protein Bars

This protein bar recipe can also be a great breakfast fare. It is easy to recreate in your own kitchen. It is jam-packed with a lot of antioxidants with blueberries.

Preparation Time: 30 Minutes

Servings: 10

Ingredients:

- 1 cup almond butter
- 1/4 cup unsweetened applesauce
- 1/3 cup honey
- 1/4 cup sunflower seeds
- 1/3 cup pepitas
- 1/3 cup walnuts
- 1/3 cup ground flaxseed
- 1/2 cup pistachios
- 1/2 cup dried blueberries
- 3/4 cup whole almonds
- 1 and 1/2 cups rolled oats

Directions:

Line a baking pan with parchment paper and set aside.

Combine the rolled oats, almonds, blueberries, pistachios, flaxseed, walnuts, pepitas, and sunflower seeds.

Add the honey and applesauce to the mixture then combine well.

Add the almond butter to the mixture.

Place the batter in the pan and press firmly.

Allow the pan to freeze overnight.

Slice into bars.

35. Strawberry Protein Bars

This protein bar is a great snack that you can eat after a workout or doing some strenuous activity. It will provide you with the energy that you need as well as the protein that your muscles need in order to repair damaged muscles.

Preparation Time: 20 Minutes

Servings: 10

Ingredients:

- 2/3 cup dark chocolate
- 1 tablespoon coconut milk
- 1/2 teaspoon vanilla
- 3 ounces unflavored whey protein
- 3 ounces unsweetened coconut, shredded
- 3 ounces freeze-dried strawberries

Directions:

Place the strawberries in a food processor and pulse until ground. Add the whey protein, coconut, and vanilla. Process until smooth.

Add the coconut milk and process until smooth.

Pour the mixture into a baking pan lined with parchment paper.

Cover and refrigerate until firm. Slice into bars.

Melt the chocolate and let it cool slightly before coating the bars with chocolate.

36. Ginger Vanilla Protein Bar

It is a warmly spiced protein bar that is packed with protein that you need to help repair damaged muscles after a hard workout.

Preparation Time: 20 Minutes

Servings: 10

Ingredients:

- 1/4 cup shredded coconut
- 1/2 cup crystallized ginger, chopped
- 1/4 cup sunflower seeds
- 1/2 cup chopped raw almonds
- 1 cup corn flakes, pounded
- 1 cup oats
- 2 scoops protein powder
- 1/4 cup coconut milk
- 1/4 cup maple syrup
- 2 tablespoons butter

Directions:

Whisk butter and syrup in a saucepan heated over medium-low heat. Add the milk and protein powder until smooth.

In another pan, combine oats, almonds, corn flakes, sunflower seeds and 3/4 of the ginger pieces.

Pour the melted butter mixture to the dry ingredients. Mix well.

Place the mixture in a baking dish lined with parchment paper.

Spread the mixture and flatten the surface by hand.

Sprinkle shredded coconut and the remaining ginger pieces on top of the mixture.

Bake for 20 minutes in a 325°F preheated oven.

Let it cool before cutting into squares.

Conclusion

Everyone needs a healthy, nutritious diet. Not only does it give us the energy that we need to perform our daily activities, but it also helps us stay healthy and live longer. A healthy diet incorporates a variety of nutritious foods that are rich in nutrients and low in fat. Protein powder is available in different forms, such as bars, cookies, smoothies, and shakes. Most of these protein powders come with a label that highlights the number of grams of protein they contain.

Homemade protein bar recipes are a great way to make your own healthy protein powder. These bars are made with nuts and fruits blended with protein powder. They taste the same as protein bars sold on the market, but they contain almost no oil or sugar, so they can be consumed by those trying to lose weight.

Try these homemade protein bar recipes, and let me know how they turned out.

About the Author

Owen isn't your typical cookbook writer. He built a life and career as a successful stockbroker in New York for many years, getting into the routine of it all. He enjoyed the crazy schedule, his exploding inbox, and endless phone conversations with clients. Still, he always found himself in the kitchen when he had some time to spare. Even if he got home at 11:00 pm and had an early morning meeting the next day, he always cooked delicious meals and dinners for himself.

When the pandemic hit and lots of his clients started pulling out, Owen began to question whether he would even have a job within the next couple of months. Once the world went into lockdown, his job became harder with the sudden obstacles of working from home with a job like his. His stress, however, was very fruitful because it often resulted in new dishes.

More than a home office, at one point, his place felt more like a restaurant. Whether it was breakfast, lunch, or dinner, he was always whipping up something amazing! When he was let go, he was relieved to finally have more time to work on new recipes to share with his friends and family. Eventually, they encouraged him to start writing cookbooks… and that's how he began his new life as an amateur cook and cookbook writer. Now, he travels across the US searching for inspiration for his recipes, but he always finds his way back home to his cozy townhouse in New Jersey, ready to share all of his new dishes with his loved ones.

Appendices

Hey, guys! I just wanted to say thanks for supporting me by purchasing one of my e-books. I have to say—when I first started writing cookbooks, I didn't have many expectations for myself because it was never a part of "the plan." It was more of a hobby, something I did for me and decided to put out there if someone might click on my book and buy it because they liked my food. Well, let me just say it's been a while since those days, and it's been a wild journey!

Now, cookbook writing is a huge part of my life, and I'm doing things I love! So, THANK YOU for trusting me with your weekly meal preps, weekend BBQs, 10-minute dinners, and all of your special occasions. If it weren't for you, I wouldn't be able to concentrate on producing all sorts of delicious recipes, which is why I've decided to reach out and ask for your help. What kind of recipes would you like to see more of? Are you interested in special diets, foods made with kitchen appliances, or just easy recipes on a time-crunch? Your input will help me create books you want to read with recipes you'll actually make! Make sure to let me know, and your suggestions could trigger an idea for my next book…

Take care!

Owen

73684235R00052

Honeybee

FABRIC	PIECE	6" BLOCK	12" BLOCK
Background (white)	A	4 squares, 1½" × 1½"	4 squares, 2½" × 2½"
	B	36 squares, 1" × 1"	36 squares, 1½" × 1½"
	C	4 rectangles, ¾" × 1¾"	4 rectangles, 1" × 3"
	D	2 rectangles, 1" × 2"	2 rectangles, 1½" × 3½"
	E	4 rectangles, ¾" × 3¼"	4 rectangles, 1" × 6"
	F	2 rectangles, ¾" × 3½"	2 rectangles, 1" × 6½"
	G	2 rectangles, 1" × 1¾"	2 rectangles, 1½" × 3"
Honeybees (yellow)	H	12 squares, 1¾" × 1¾"	12 squares, 3" × 3"
Nine Patch (orange plaid)	I	5 squares, 1½" × 1½"	5 squares, 2½" × 2½"

MAKING THE BLOCK

Instructions are for both 6" and 12" blocks. Sew all pieces right sides together. When layering pieces marked with a diagonal line, stitch on the marked line. Trim the seam allowances to ¼". Press all seam allowances open to reduce bulk.

1. Draw a diagonal line on the wrong side of the B squares. Sew B to the top-left corner of H. Sew B to the top-right and bottom-left corners of H. Make 12 H units.

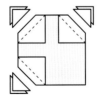

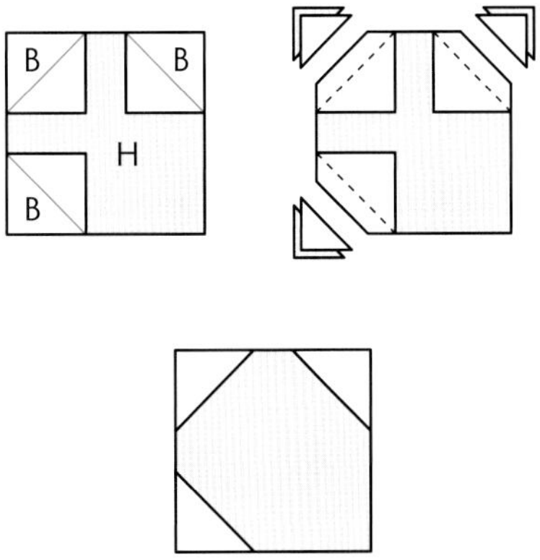

Make 12 units.

2. Sew C between two H units. Add E. Make four units.

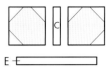

Make 4 units.

3. Sew D between two units from step 2. Make two rows.

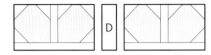

Make 2 rows.

4. Sew G between two H units. Add F to make a side unit. Make two.

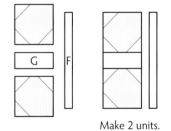

Make 2 units.

5. Join A and I squares to make a nine-patch unit.

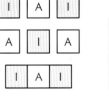

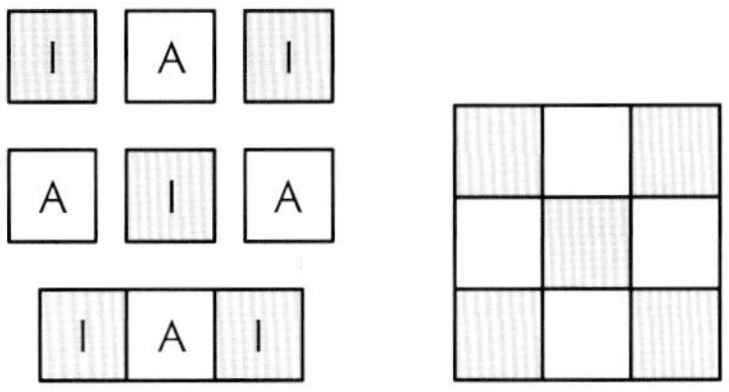

Make 1 unit.

6. Join the units to make the center row. Join the rows to make the block.

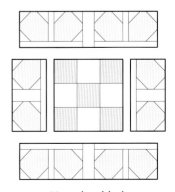

Honeybee block

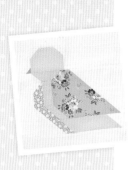

Acknowledgments

I want to acknowledge my great-grandma, Barbara-Lee Summers, who began our family quilting legacy, and my grandma, Rita Pickering, who taught me how to quilt and opened a whole new world to me.

A huge thank-you to Annie Seaboch (Annie Leigh's Sew Happy) for your beautiful long-arm quilting!

About the Author

Gracey Larson lives in beautiful, rural East Tennessee with her dad and mom, her two sisters, her brother, a bunny, and 10 chickens. When asked how long she has been a maker, Gracey says that she has been creating since she was old enough to hold a crayon. She has always enjoyed living in a world of color, pattern, and creativity. Gracey began quilting in 2009, after years of admiring her great-grandmother's quilts, and quilting has been an ongoing passion for her ever since.

As a Christian and self-described "wildflower," Gracey loves God, her family, her church family, adventure, traveling and singing with her family, and stitching those memories and moments into her quilts. Her patterns are unique and whimsical, and they appeal to a growing number of quilters who seek to include pictures in their own projects without the need for paper piecing or templates. Gracey's work has also appeared in *Love Patchwork & Quilting* magazine.